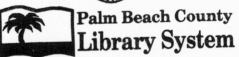

FOCUS: *Five Women Photographers*

FOCUS: *Five Women Photographers*

JULIA MARGARET CAMERON

MARGARET BOURKE-WHITE

FLOR GARDUÑO

SANDY SKOGLUND

LORNA SIMPSON

Sylvia Wolf

ALBERT WHITMAN & COMPANY • MORTON GROVE, ILLINOIS

For Annie, Molly, Emily, and Nick

ALL OF US, AT ONE TIME OR ANOTHER, have taken a photograph or have had a photograph taken of us. Photography is something anyone can do with a little instruction. But to create art with a camera—to make images that capture beauty, that tell us about the world we live in, or that make us feel deep emotions—is a different thing entirely.

The five women I have written about succeed at this magnificently. As a group, they show how many different ways there are to make art with photography. As individuals, they are truly inspirational. Julia Margaret Cameron was a portrait photographer who broke all the rules of nineteenth-century photographic practice. Margaret Bourke-White was an adventurer who used the camera to report the most important world events of the 1930s through the 1950s. The other three photographers are working today. Flor Garduño preserves the timeless rituals of native Latin American cultures. Sandy Skoglund builds zany stage sets for the sole purpose of photographing them. And Lorna Simpson uses pictures and words to ask questions about prejudice and social stereotypes.

In this book, I give you my interpretation of each artist's work. But as you read, look closely at the pictures, for you may see things I do not. Let your imagination run free with the same spirit of experimentation and discovery that has shaped the lives of these five remarkable photographers.

Sylvia Wolf
Art Institute of Chicago

Contents

JULIA MARGARET CAMERON

Julia Margaret Cameron and Her Children Charles and Henry, about 1860

JULIA MARGARET CAMERON was born in Calcutta, India, on June 11, 1815. Her father, James Pattle, worked for the East India Company, a British-owned business that traded Indian products to foreign countries. Julia was the fourth of ten children.

When Julia was three, her mother, Adeline, took her and a younger sister, Sarah, to France to live with their grandmother and be educated. The sisters stayed for years. They must have missed their parents, but they loved their grandmother, and she adored them. They also loved the beauty of Versailles, the place where she lived.

Versailles is a small town outside of Paris, built around the huge castle of Louis the Fourteenth, who was king of France in the late 1600s and early 1700s. Behind the castle, deep green woods with reflecting pools, fountains, and sculpture stretch for miles. It was a wonderful place for the girls to play.

When they grew older, the sisters were free to roam. In between lessons in reading, writing, cooking, and dressmaking, Julia and Sarah wandered in the gardens of the great French palace. Along the pathways they found stone altars, hideaways, and statues of Greek gods and goddesses. They played make-believe, and they daydreamed of fairies, saints, and elves. In these magical gardens, Julia's vivid imagination flourished.

In 1834, when she was nineteen, Julia moved back to India. A year later, she met Charles Hay Cameron, an Englishman. Cameron was twenty years older than Julia. A quiet man, he was a lawyer who worked to improve Indian laws. In 1838, Charles and Julia were married.

During the ten years the Camerons lived in India, they were happy. Both enjoyed the Indian culture, and they had many friends. Julia was greatly loved for her warm heart and sense of humor. With dark, sparkling eyes and a gruff voice, she was a flamboyant storyteller and a lively hostess. It was Julia's talent at winning friendship that helped her find models for her photographs years later.

In 1848, when Julia was thirty-three, Charles retired from his job, and the Camerons moved to London, England. Later, they moved to the Isle of Wight, off England's southern coast. Over the years, Julia and Charles raised twelve children. They had six of their own (five boys and one girl). They adopted five orphans of relatives and took in a beggar girl. Julia liked having a busy household. But one by one, her children grew older, got married, and moved away.

In 1863, when her husband was on a trip to India, Julia became lonely. She was also worried about money because the Camerons were in debt. To cheer her up, her daughter and son-in-law gave her a big wooden camera. With it, she thought she might take pictures to earn extra income. Photography never made Julia rich, but it brought her pleasure for the rest of her life.

Julia was forty-eight years old when she started her first experiments with the camera. Photography had been announced to the world only twenty-four years earlier, in 1839, by a Frenchman and an Englishman who had each discovered different ways of making photographic pictures. For the first time, an image of the real world could be created that was not made by hand, like a painting or drawing. Everyone was fascinated with the science and magic of photography.

Even so, not many people took pictures. Photographic chemicals were toxic. They also smelled bad, stained clothes, and turned fingernails black. In the 1860s, photography was not considered a ladylike activity. Women were expected to spend their time overseeing their homes and families, not working with messy chemicals. But Julia was not concerned with what others thought she should or should not do. She plunged into photography with all of her energy.

First, Julia turned the glass-roofed chicken coop behind her house into a studio for taking pictures (she let all the chickens go free). Then, she changed the coal house into a darkroom. The next step was to find people to pose for her.

From the start, Julia knew she wanted to make portraits. In the 1860s, portraits of famous people were popular. These photographs were small pictures that showed a person from head to toe. The subject stood or sat in front of a painted backdrop. It was a special occasion to have a picture taken, so people got dressed up and posed with serious expressions.

Julia hated these photographs. To her, everyone in the pictures looked stiff and formal. She did not want simply to show what people looked like on the outside. She wanted her photographs to express emotion, beauty, and nobility of spirit. These were high aspirations for someone who did not yet know how to use a camera.

In the early years of photography, cameras were big and cumbersome. They did not take roll film as they do today. Instead, photographers made pictures one at a time. The film consisted of a piece of glass, called a *glass plate negative,* that was placed in the back of the camera, behind the lens. The plate had been coated with a light-sensitive chemical called an *emulsion.* It was this emulsion that reacted to light and created the photographic image.

If the photographer did not spread the emulsion evenly on the glass plate, she would get a picture with streaks. If, by mistake, she rubbed the glass before the emulsion dried, she would smudge and ruin it. Any dust or dirt on the glass would stick and show up as spots on the final picture. It was difficult even for a professional photographer to make a good glass plate. For a beginner like Julia, sometimes photography seemed impossible. But she would not give up.

After weeks of trying, Julia made the first photograph she was happy with—a portrait of a little girl named Annie Philpot. Underneath it, Julia wrote, "Annie—my first success, January 1864." Other photographers of the time would not have called it a success, however. The picture is out of focus. Annie's hair is mussed. She is not looking at the camera. With her coat buttoned up, she looks as if she has just come in from playing outside.

But these things are precisely what Julia liked about the picture. When she first saw her portrait of Annie, she knew she had done something new and different. Annie looked energetic and alive, not stuffy and self-conscious like the people in formal portraits. Julia wanted to make more photographs like this one.

First, though, she had to figure out what she had done to make this picture so she could do the same thing again. Julia thought she might not have screwed the lens tightly on the camera, and that is why her portrait of Annie was out of focus. But there were other reasons. Julia's glass plates were nine by eleven inches, the size used for landscape photography, instead of four by four and one-half inches, the standard size for mid-nineteenth-century portraits. It was impossible to keep everything in focus on such a big plate. Also, with large pictures, it takes a long time to make an *exposure*—the photographic term for what happens when light makes an image on the film. Julia's exposures took between three and seven minutes. When models breathed, the slight movement from the breathing was recorded as a blur on film.

Julia could have corrected these things, but she chose not to. Instead, she broke all the rules

Annie, My First Success, 1864

Sir John Herschel, 1867

of photographic practice, for her vision of what a portrait should be was strong. In the 1860s, people loved photography because the camera could make a precise likeness of a subject. Good portraits were sharp and clear, and they were small, precious things. But Julia's portraits were big, and soft in focus. They were unlike anything anyone had ever seen before.

With her unusual style, Julia made numerous portraits of famous people. In 1867, she photographed the chemist and royal astronomer Sir John Herschel, who had been her friend for many years. First, she asked him to wash his hair and let it dry freely so that he would look natural for the picture. She moved the camera as close to him as she could so that his face would take up the entire picture. Then she asked him to look directly at the camera and to keep his eyes wide open. In the photograph, Herschel stares at us with great concentration. The overhead lighting from the glass-roofed chicken coop adds to the drama of the picture. Julia succeeded in portraying the intensity and the electric energy of this great scientist.

Julia persuaded other famous people to pose for her. She met some of her subjects through her sister Sarah, who knew them from social events. Among them were the painter George Frederick Watts, the scientist Charles Darwin, and the poets Robert Browning, Henry Wadsworth

Longfellow, and Alfred, Lord Tennyson, her neighbor and close friend.

For Tennyson's portrait, Julia draped a dark cloth over the poet's shoulders to cover up his everyday clothes. She believed that clothes tell too much about a person's social class and about the fashions of the time. To her, Tennyson's writings were timeless; therefore, he should be, too. She turned him to the side and placed a book in his hand. The poet looks wistful and dreamy. Tennyson liked Julia's portrait so much that he often posed for her again.

Julia worked for hours on a single portrait. When she made a print she was happy with, she rushed back to the house to show it to her husband, often dripping photography chemicals on the lawn, floor, and carpets. The smell of chemicals was everywhere. At that time, photographic prints were made by coating a piece of paper with light-sensitive chemicals, putting the paper face down on the glass plate negative, and setting the two in the sun for the exposure. At Julia's house, the frames that held the photo paper and glass plate negative together were scattered all over the yard. It was hard for members of her household to get used to the mess. But they could see how much photography meant to Julia. They could also see that there was no stopping her.

In the late 1860s and early 1870s, Julia made

Alfred Tennyson, 1865

more than five hundred photographs. Her work became well known through exhibitions in London and Paris, and she won a gold medal at an international exhibition in Berlin. Even so, some successful photographers did not take her seriously. They called her a "lady amateur," and they criticized her photographs because they were out of focus and often scratched or streaked. It is true that Julia was not a good technician. But she did not intend to make a sharp, perfect picture. It was the mood, the overall effect, she was looking for. To her, what she photographed was deeply beautiful.

The painters and writers who were Julia's friends agreed with her. They did not compare her pictures to other photographs of the time. They looked at her portraits as works of art, and they encouraged her. Many belonged to the Pre-Raphaelite painting movement, whose members painted famous scenes from literature, religion, and mythology.

Julia was influenced by the work of the Pre-Raphaelites and some of her photographs are similar in spirit to their paintings. Unlike her portraits of famous men, who were pictured as themselves, Julia depicted women as goddesses, saints, and heroines of great literature. In the late 1800s, women had long hair that they wore in braids and buns pinned to their heads. They only let their hair down when they went to sleep.

For her photographs, Julia asked women to unpin their hair. She believed this would make them look more like the characters they were playing in her pictures.

In one image, Julia posed Alice Liddell, the girl that the story *Alice in Wonderland* was written for, as Pomona, the Greek goddess of the fruits of trees. Paintings of Pomona usually show her surrounded by fertile gardens, so Julia's Pomona stands against a wall covered with flowering vines. Her hair is draped over her shoulders, and she gazes directly at the camera.

One of Julia's most emotional photographs (see p. 14) shows a profile of a woman who is wrapped in a dark cloth. As a title, she added the phrase "Call, I follow, I follow, let me die!" (The line comes from a poem she loved by Tennyson.) It is the sweeping motion of the hair and the look of longing on the model's face that bring the drama of the poem to life.

Tennyson liked these theatrical pictures so much that in 1874, he asked Julia if she would make photographs to illustrate a collection of his poems about King Arthur and the Knights of the Round Table. Julia loved the idea, and she got to work.

For this project, she chose her models based on how they looked, not on who they were. Even her parlor maids were asked to pose. She positioned her models to mimic what Tennyson

Pomona, 1872

Call, I follow, I follow, let me die! about 1867

had written. Her childhood days of play-acting in the gardens of Versailles had prepared her for this imaginative work.

The job, however, was tough. Julia made almost two hundred photographs in order to get twelve good pictures. In 1874, these photographs were published in Tennyson's book *Idylls of the King*. This was one of the last groups of photographs Julia made before she left England.

In 1875, Julia and Charles moved to Ceylon (now Sri Lanka), an island off the southern coast of India. After the Camerons arrived, Julia made a few photographs of Indian women carrying water bottles or sitting in outdoor gardens. But she did not photograph with the same spirit or determination as she had in England. Perhaps it was because photo chemicals of the time did not work well in the heat and humidity of Ceylon. Or maybe photography was not exciting to her once she was away from the family and friends who had posed for her in the past. Whatever the reason, Julia made only a few photographs after she left England. Four years after she moved to Ceylon, she died, at age sixty-three. Charles died the following year.

A little over a decade later, Julia's style of photography became popular among a group of American and European photographers called the Pictorialists. They wanted to make photographs that expressed emotion, not pictures that showed in detail what something looked like. They were interested in the same things Julia had cared about. Still, she was the pioneer. She had the imagination to make a new kind of photograph and the courage to stand by her ideals. Historians now recognize Julia Margaret Cameron as one of the great portrait photographers of the nineteenth century.

Ceylon, about 1875

MARGARET BOURKE-WHITE

Margaret Bourke-White in High-Altitude Flying Suit, 1943

When she was young, MARGARET BOURKE-WHITE's best friends were the garter snakes she caught in the woods near her house. Margaret was a quiet girl—too serious to be popular with other children. But when she took her snakes to school, her classmates thought she was wonderfully strange. Margaret liked being different. She once wrote in her diary that she pictured herself "doing all the things that women never do."

Margaret Bourke-White was born to Minnie and Joseph White in the Bronx, New York, on June 14, 1904. (Margaret added Minnie's maiden name, Bourke, when she started her career in photography.) Margaret's mother was an avid reader with an adventurous spirit. She taught Margaret and her younger brother and sister to be curious, determined, and fearless. Her father was a mechanical engineer and inventor who worked for a printing company. He felt that hard work and striving for perfection were the highest human virtues. When Margaret was faced with a tough task, he would urge her to keep trying. "*You can,*" he would say.

When Margaret was eight years old, her father took her on a tour of a foundry, a place where iron and other materials are melted at very high temperatures to make steel. (The steel is then shaped into machine parts.) Margaret watched with fascination as flames jumped from the bubbling vats of molten steel. In the heat, noise, and fiery light of the foundry, she saw beauty and power. When Margaret became a photographer, her first and favorite subjects were factories and machines.

Margaret was introduced to photography by her father, an amateur photographer. As a young girl, she often helped him in his darkroom. When her father died during her first year in college, Margaret decided to pursue photography on her own. Apart from her science courses at Columbia University in New York City, she took classes at the Clarence White School of Photography.

Everett Chapman, another student at Columbia, shared her interest in the camera. Over time, the two fell in love. In 1924, Margaret left school, and she and Everett were married.

At first, Margaret and Everett seemed to be a perfect match. They both loved photography, science, and machines. They had fun together, and they made each other laugh. But Everett was possessive of Margaret, and Everett's mother was possessive of Everett. Margaret had difficulty maintaining her independence and peace of mind within the marriage. She and Everett tried hard to make the marriage work, but after two years, they separated. In 1928, they were divorced.

Margaret was deeply saddened by the breakup, but she was determined to rise above her troubles. Right away, she re-enrolled in school to study science, this time at Cornell University in Ithaca, New York. (Margaret attended five schools during her college years.) To help pay her living expenses, she took architectural photographs of the university's buildings and sold them to students, faculty, and the alumni magazine. Margaret loved taking pictures, and the photographs sold well. Soon she decided that photography would be her life's work.

When she was twenty-three, Margaret moved to Cleveland, Ohio, in the hopes of getting a job as an architectural photographer. A booming industrial city, Cleveland was the perfect place for

Blast Furnace Operator with "Mud Gun," Otis Steel Company, about 1927-28

someone who loved buildings and factory machinery. Margaret made many photographs in the Otis Steel Company's foundries. In one, light shines behind cables, pipes, and a man bending over at work. The silhouettes in the hot, misty air give the scene a mysterious, exciting feeling. To make a picture like this, Margaret often stood so close to steam and molten steel that factory workers were afraid she might get burned. They tried to make her stay back, but Margaret would not listen. When it came to getting a picture she wanted, no one could stand in her way.

Henry Luce, publisher of *Time* magazine, saw Margaret's Otis Steel photographs and thought they were terrific. Luce was founding a new magazine, called *Fortune*. It would be the first to use photographs to bring industry and big business to life. Luce offered Margaret a job photographing for *Fortune* magazine, and she accepted.

Margaret quickly became known for taking pictures no woman—and few men—had taken before. During the winter months of 1929-30, she photographed construction work at the top of New York City's Chrysler Building as the skyscraper was being built. Eight hundred feet up, in cold wind, she teetered on a scaffold with her camera and tripod as the building swayed.

Margaret used a large, heavy camera that took four-by-five-inch negatives. Smaller cameras were available, but they took long, rectangular images. Margaret preferred the sharp detail and the broad, almost square images that she got with a bigger negative. Image quality was important to Margaret and, for her, working with large-format cameras was the only way to get the striking compositions she loved so much.

When the Chrysler Building was finished, Margaret rented a studio behind the stainless steel gargoyles that decorated the top of the building. She liked to climb out on the gargoyles and photograph the city below. Amazed by Margaret's fearlessness, newspaper and magazine reporters wrote about her daring. The stories were not just about her photographs—they were about *her*. Margaret Bourke-White was becoming a celebrity.

In 1930, Margaret proposed to *Fortune* that she photograph the factories being built throughout the Soviet Union. But the Soviet government did not permit foreigners to travel freely around the country taking pictures. This made Margaret all the more determined to go. She once said, "Nothing attracts me like a closed door. I cannot let my camera rest until I have pried it open." Margaret finally persuaded Soviet officials to let her photograph wherever she wished. Through her pictures, Americans got their first glimpse of the developing industry of the Soviet Union.

In the 1930s and 1940s, people learned about news and world events from the radio, newspapers, and magazines. Television was being developed, but it was not on the market yet. As one of the main photographers for America's finest photographic magazine, Margaret Bourke-White helped viewers see and understand events in other parts of the world. She was also one of the toughest and most talented photographers in the business. In a pretty dress with matching hat and gloves (Margaret loved fashionable clothes), she would push her way through a crowd or travel halfway around the world to get a good picture.

The photographs published in *Fortune* were so popular that its founders decided to start another magazine—one with even more photographs. The magazine, named *Life,* contained very little writing. Instead, in a new format called the "photographic essay," it let the pictures tell the story. Margaret joined *Life* when the magazine was formed in 1936 and was the only woman among the magazine's first four staff photographers. Except for a short time working for a daily newspaper in 1940, she stayed with *Life* until she retired twenty-one years later.

For its first issue, *Life* sent Margaret to photograph the Fort Peck Dam in Montana. The dam was being built as part of President Franklin D. Roosevelt's effort to boost America's economy after the Depression. In one of Margaret's

Dam at Fort Peck, Montana, 1936

photographs, the dam looks like a fortress. Two tiny men at the bottom of the image give the structure a sense of scale and magnitude. The image seems to say that through technology and new building projects, the country would leave the Depression behind and be strong and solid again. This photograph was used on the cover of *Life*'s first issue on November 23, 1936.

That same year, when she was thirty-two, Margaret met Erskine Caldwell, a well-known American novelist who wrote about poverty, racial tension, and the struggles of daily life in rural America. Margaret liked his writing, and he admired her photographs. Soon after they met, they decided to do a project that they believed would draw attention to the thousands of families in the United States who lived in poverty. Off and on for a year, they traveled around the country photographing and interviewing America's poor.

One of Margaret's pictures is of a young boy whose growth was stunted by disease and malnutrition. To keep out the cold, the walls of the room he sits in have been covered by magazine and newspaper pages. The pages advertise cars and expensive insurance—things the boy's family could not afford. This photograph and others Margaret took showed readers all over the country what despair, poverty, and pride looked like on the faces of poor Americans. In the late 1930s and early 1940s, images like this one

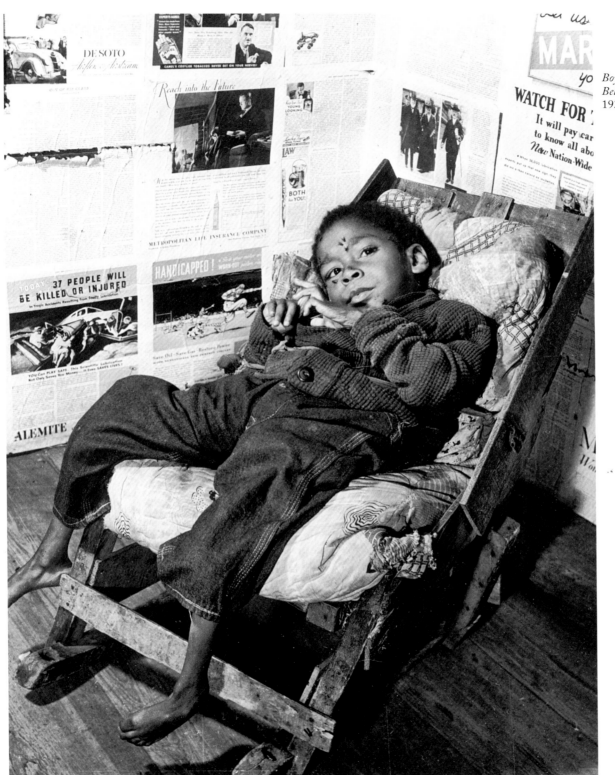

Boy in Chair,
Belmont, Florida,
1936-37

helped win popular support for government programs to aid families in need.

In 1937, Margaret's pictures and Erskine's writings were published in a book called *You Have Seen Their Faces*. During this project, the two fell in love, and in 1939 they were married. Over the next three years, Margaret and Erskine published two more books. *North of the Danube* (1939) was an account of their travels in Czechoslovakia during the summer of 1938, the year before World War II began. *Say, is this the U.S.A.*, published in 1941, showed what everyday life looked like in small towns across America.

In May 1941, Margaret and Erskine returned to the Soviet Union. World War II was underway in Europe, and on June 22, German troops invaded the Soviet Union from the west. Less than a month later, on the night of July 19, Margaret was the only foreign photographer in Moscow when the Germans attacked. As bombs fell on the city, she climbed to the rooftop of the American embassy to take pictures.

Margaret was not concerned for her safety. Instead, she worried about getting good photographs. How would she expose for the black of night and the blinding white of the explosions? How would she know where the next bomb would hit so she could aim her camera? Using all of the skill and instincts she had developed as a photographer, Margaret made spectacular pictures of shells splashing across Moscow's night sky.

Soon after their trip to the Soviet Union, Margaret and Erskine grew apart, and in 1942, they were divorced. Again Margaret lost herself in her work, this time by photographing scenes of war throughout Europe. As she did, the legend of Margaret Bourke-White grew. Readers of *Life* eagerly followed Margaret's adventures. She survived when her ship was torpedoed and sunk in the Mediterranean. She went on a secret bombing mission. And she leaped from an army jeep just before it was hit by enemy shells. Like a cat with nine lives, Margaret always bounced back. She had the two most important things for being a successful news photographer: good timing and extraordinary luck.

Early in 1945, Margaret photographed a famous American, Gen. George S. Patton, in Germany. Then she followed his troops as they pursued retreating German forces. On April 11 of that year, Patton's regiment arrived at Buchenwald, one of many concentration camps built by the Nazis. In these camps alone, the Germans killed over four million Jews, along with gypsies and political prisoners.

Buchenwald was the first major concentration camp any American troops had seen, and what they found was shocking. Hundreds and hundreds of naked dead bodies lay piled in stacks. Other prisoners were barely alive. All had been forced

Buchenwald, Germany, the Day after Liberation, April 1945

Gandhi, India, 1946

into slave labor and starved. Ovens that had been built to incinerate thousands of dead prisoners a day contained bone fragments and ashes from the last bodies burned.

At first, it was difficult for Margaret to take pictures, but she knew that without photographs, people would not believe reports of the horror at Buchenwald. She set up her camera and got to work. One image is of inmates lined up behind a barbed wire fence, staring blankly at the camera. These men have seen so much death and brutality that they have little spirit left. Although physically they are alive, they seem emotionally dead. Photographs like these shocked the American public. Few who saw them will ever forget them.

A year later, with the war ended, Margaret was sent to document India's struggle for independence from Great Britain. India's great peace leader, Mahatma Gandhi, agreed to pose for her. First, though, Gandhi's secretary insisted Margaret take a lesson in spinning cotton so that she could understand the Mahatma's philosophy. To Gandhi, the spinning wheel represented India's break from Britain. He believed that cotton grown in India should be spun there, not in British textile mills, as was done at the time. When Margaret photographed Gandhi, she positioned his spinning wheel in the foreground of the portrait. It fills almost half the frame. By giving it so much space and importance, she reminds us of

Gandhi's desire for India to be free from British rule.

Margaret returned to India in 1947 for a photographic study of Indian culture. In 1949, her images were published in a book called *Halfway to Freedom*, a title that describes India's struggle for independence. While working on the book, Margaret saw brutal fighting between Muslims and Hindus, two Indian religious groups who each wanted their own territory. The conflict eventually split the country. In August 1947, India achieved independence from Britain and was divided into two parts: India, a Hindu state, and Pakistan, a Muslim nation.

Even after the division, violence continued. Gandhi tried to put a stop to the religious battles. In January 1948 he announced that he would fast (he would not eat) until the fighting stopped. Gandhi came close to dying of starvation before the warring groups agreed to a truce. A few days later, however, he was killed by a Hindu who opposed his efforts for peace.

When Gandhi's body was laid out for mourners to view, Margaret was told she could enter, *without* her cameras. But always looking for a scoop, she sneaked a camera in and tried to take pictures. Immediately, she was thrown out. At Gandhi's public funeral, where his body was cremated before thousands of mourners, Margaret tried to photograph again. But the crowd jostled her, and she was unable to keep the camera steady for the exposure. It was rare for Margaret to miss getting a photograph she wanted.

Although she was always where the action was, Margaret was not an action photographer. Other "photojournalists" used small, hand-held cameras that could take spontaneous, quick pictures. Margaret, however, still preferred her big, heavy camera and tripod. Before taking a photo, she had to set up the equipment. This was hard to do when events happened quickly. But to Margaret, it was worth the extra effort to get the large negative and crisp detail that she preferred, even if, as at Gandhi's funeral, she occasionally missed a shot or two.

In late 1949, Margaret was sent to do a photographic essay on racial injustice in South Africa, where whites, who were in the minority, brutally mistreated native Africans. She traveled two miles underground into a gold mine to photograph men who did hard and dangerous work for little pay. These men were known not by their names, but by numbers tattooed on their arms. In Margaret's photograph, #1139 and #5122 stand facing the camera. Their sweat shimmers in the artificial light of Margaret's flash. She positioned the camera to fill the frame with their torsos. In spite of miserable conditions and racial oppression, the workers appear noble and monumental.

This picture and ones Margaret made during the Korean War in the early fifties are among the last of her career. In 1954, when she was forty-nine, Margaret was diagnosed with Parkinson's disease, an illness that attacks the nervous system. She continued to work for *Life* until 1957. Then, for fourteen years, she fought Parkinson's disease with the same bravery and determination that had made her a great photographer. In 1971, at age sixty-six, Margaret died of her illness.

During her years with *Life*, Margaret Bourke-White's photographs were seen by over one hundred million viewers each year. Today, they are admired both as historical documents and as works of art; they can be found in history textbooks and in museum collections around the world. She became a legendary figure in photography and paved the way for future photojournalists, men and women alike. Margaret succeeded many times over in fulfilling her childhood dream of doing things women of her time did not do. She never forgot her mother's lessons in curiosity and fearlessness and her father's words *"You can."*

Gold Miners,
Johannesburg,
South Africa,
1950

FLOR GARDUÑO

Flor Garduño
in 1986

FLOR GARDUÑO was born the youngest of three children in Mexico City, Mexico, on March 21, 1957. Her mother, Estela, was a merchant, and her father, Gregorio, was a civil engineer. When Flor was five years old, her family moved to a farm outside of Mexico City. Flor's father had a strong love for animals and for life in the country. He often took the children on walks and pointed out animals, beautiful flowers, and fruit. It was from him that Flor developed her appreciation of nature.

From the time Flor was a girl, she knew she

wanted to be an artist. At age eighteen, she left home to enter the San Carlos School of Fine Arts in Mexico City. For three years, she studied painting and drawing and read poetry, literature, and philosophy. She went to see films, sometimes two in one day. Then the teachers went on strike. Flor was anxious to keep learning, so she signed up to study with the only teacher who was not on strike, a photographer named Kati Horna.

Before then, Flor had not been interested in photography. She had watched photographers on the streets of Mexico City who took portraits of people for a few pesos. But their work looked boring to Flor. It was not until she studied with Kati Horna that Flor discovered how wonderful photography could be.

Horna was a Hungarian photographer who had moved to Mexico City during the Second World War. In Europe, she had been friends with many important artists who were pioneers of modern art. Horna considered photography to be a fine art equal to painting and sculpture. She taught her students that an artist's first task is to develop good ideas. The next step is to figure out the right technique for expressing those ideas. Horna was passionate about photography, and her enthusiasm was contagious. Flor and the other students were in awe of her.

Flor showed Horna pictures she had taken in an abandoned shop where dolls had been repaired.

In her photographs, the broken arms, legs, and torsos of dolls were piled high in a darkened room. The images were moody and mysterious. Horna liked the feeling of the photographs, and she began to pay special attention to Flor.

Horna taught Flor about composition. She explained that what is left out of a picture is as important in making a strong photograph as what is included in the frame. She showed how lighting defines the feeling of a picture and how sunlight, candlelight, and camera flash each produce a different effect. Horna taught Flor that if she made technical choices carefully and thoughtfully, she would end up making better pictures. While learning from Horna, Flor became spellbound by photography. When the teachers' strike was over, she gave up her studies in painting to keep taking classes with this inspiring teacher.

Through Horna, Flor came to know the work of other photographers, including Manuel Alvarez Bravo, the master of Mexican photography. One day, a friend of Flor's took her to meet Alvarez Bravo. Flor asked if she could watch him work in the darkroom. She knew that making beautiful prints was as much an art as taking the picture, and she wanted to see how the great photographer worked. The two got along well, and Alvarez Bravo hired Flor as his assistant. While continuing her studies, she worked for the Mexican master for two years. Assisting Alvarez Bravo made her

Kings of Canes, Tulancingo, Mexico, 1981

realize she wanted to devote her life to photography. When Flor was twenty-two, she left school to work as a photographer.

Flor's first job was with the Mexican secretary of public education. Her assignment was to visit and photograph in remote villages throughout Mexico where native Indians lived. Before the sixteenth century, when Spanish conquerors arrived in Latin America (Mexico, Central America, and South America), this area was inhabited by native Indians. From region to region, they had different languages and cultures. Today, over forty million Indians occupy villages all over Latin America. They still speak native languages, and they maintain many of their old customs. Other customs are mixed with the Christian practices brought by the Spaniards.

In these Indian communities, Flor's task was to take pictures of everyday activities. Later, the photographs appeared in children's schoolbooks written in native languages as well as Mexico's national language, Spanish. The images were used to illustrate words and help children learn how to read and write.

One of these early pictures is of two brothers walking home from the fields in Tulancingo, Mexico. Each one carries a huge squash over his shoulder like a baseball bat. The squash has been dried and hollowed out to be used as a tool for getting sap out of the agave plant. The sap is then used to make *pulque*, once the sacred drink of the Aztec people, who ruled an empire in Mexico in the fifteenth and early sixteenth centuries. *(Pulque* is now made as a liquor, not a sacred drink.) In the photograph, the boys look one way, and the squashes tilt the other. The bold but simple composition makes this a dynamic picture.

Flor worked for the secretary of education for two years. After that, she photographed sculptures and paintings for art books. Then an exciting thing happened. Francisco Toledo, one of Mexico's famous painters and a friend of Flor's, offered to publish a book of her photographs. He liked her pictures and thought other people would like them, too. This was a great honor.

Flor selected her favorite photographs for the book. One is of a dense cloud of hundreds of birds flying above a country farm. Flor had seen them from a distance as they landed in the trees. They were so beautiful that she drove closer and loaded her film as quickly as she could. She hoped to photograph the birds as they flew away. Just as she was ready, they took flight. Flor had barely enough time to take one quick picture before they were gone.

Flor's equipment made it possible for her to act spontaneously in taking this picture. Her cameras are smaller and lighter than the ones used by Julia Margaret Cameron or Margaret Bourke-White. Also, her film speed is fast. This allowed

Cloud, Jocotitlán, Mexico, 1982

31

her to stop the birds' motion as they flew. Even so, she knew she was lucky. It is difficult to be in the right place at the right time. When that happens and Flor takes a picture she is happy with, she says it is one of the best feelings in the world.

When Flor's book, *Magic of the Eternal Game*, was published in 1985, she took it to the international book fair in Frankfurt, Germany. One company there liked her work so much that they asked her to publish a book with them. She proposed one on animals. (Flor has loved animals since her childhood days on the farm.) The company liked the idea, and she got started.

With the book in mind, Flor made a photograph of a woman holding iguanas. She first saw the woman in the marketplace in a little town in Mexico where iguanas are caught in the rocks and cooked for food. Although many people in the marketplace sold iguanas, it is this particular woman that Flor chose to photograph. She loved the woman's hair. It was as thick as a tree, Flor says. She was also drawn to the woman's hypnotic presence. Flor positioned her against a dark background so that nothing would take attention from her long black hair and the string of live iguanas she held. In the photograph, the iguanas look like an extension of the woman's flowing hair.

In all native cultures, animals have a special place in society. For example, before the Spanish brought Christianity to Latin America, the Indian gods took the form of animals. The jaguar was a symbol of, or stood for, one of the Mayan gods. (The Maya ruled in southern Mexico and Central America through much of the third to the sixteenth centuries.) The eagle symbolized one of the Aztec gods.

Today, many Indian towns hold a yearly festival to honor the native gods. In the Mexican town of Jalpán, a traveling dance troupe sets up a pole in the town square. Over thirty feet in height, it is only eight to twelve inches in diameter. Four dancers hang and spin in circles from ropes attached high up on the pole. Each represents one of the four cardinal points—North, South, East, and West. A fifth dancer leads the group. All five are dressed as the eagle knight, a figure from Aztec mythology. The lead dancer climbs to the top of the pole and performs a dance called the *Palo Voladar,* a ritual dance of thanks for good weather to the town's patron saint. Because the pole is so tall and narrow, the dancer on top must have great courage and skill.

In 1986, Flor visited Jalpán at the time of the festival. When the dance was over, she photographed the lead dancer in his eagle knight costume, which was a coat of feathers and a helmet in the shape of an eagle's head. Flor moved him away from the other dancers and the crowd. She then turned him to the side to get the view of the mask that makes the man look most

The Woman, Juchitán, Mexico, 1987

Eagle Knight,
Jalpán, Mexico, 1986

like a bird. In doing so, she suggests how the costumed man is a symbol of the Aztec god.

Flor took many pictures of people wearing animal masks or costumes in religious ceremonies. In Bolivia, she photographed a man in a painted metal mask with porcupine quills. It represented the face of a wolf cub. To take the picture, Flor moved in close, so the mask would fill the frame. The man's eyes looking out at us make the mask seem to come alive.

Flor included the eagle dancer and the woman with the iguanas in her book *Bestiarium* (the Latin word for collection of animals), which was published in 1987. She also added writings about animals by Mexican authors. Together, the words and pictures show the power of animal imagery in Latin American culture.

While working on *Bestiarium,* Flor traveled with Adriano Heitmann, a Swiss journalist and photographer. Like Flor, he was interested in the Indian cultures of Latin America, and he had helped her plan the book. Over time, Flor and Adriano fell in love.

During the next few years, they visited Guatemala, Ecuador, Bolivia, Peru, and tiny villages throughout Mexico. One picture she took in Guatemala celebrates the beauty of nature and light. Flor was driving along a small country road when she saw a girl, about ten or twelve years old, walking with a basket of lilies balanced on her

Sixto, Altos de la Paz, Bolivia, 1990

Basket of Light,
Sumpango, Guatemala,
1989

head. The girl wore the traditional dress of the area. Flor followed the girl to her house, then asked if she could take a picture. By positioning the girl half in shadow, half in light, she made a striking composition. The lilies shine in the sunlight like a floral crown.

In 1992, Flor published her third book, *Witnesses of Time*. The book became an instant hit. It won a Kodak award as one of the best photography books of 1992 and was translated from Spanish into five languages. That same year, an exhibition of photographs from the book began a tour of museums in Europe and the United States.

Flor's photographs are popular because they are stunning pictures as well as documents of timeless traditions. Though modern technology has come to many villages, native Indians have maintained their heritage. With the camera, Flor shows us the survival of Indian cultures in Latin America.

A year after *Witnesses of Time* was published, Flor gave birth to her first child, a baby girl named Azul. Today, Flor, her husband, Adriano, and Azul divide their time between two homes. For part of the year, they live in a small white house in the foothills of the Swiss Alps. For the rest, they live in the Mexican village of Tepoztlán. Flor will continue making pictures, and she may even return to painting someday. In the meantime, however, she is enjoying the success of her most recent book and her days and nights with Azul.

SANDY SKOGLUND

Sandy Skoglund
at work in 1991

SANDY SKOGLUND has always been good at making things. As a girl, she created comic books, designed dresses for her dolls, and sewed her own clothes. She was especially good at drawing caricatures of people. To amuse her friends, Sandy often made cartoons spoofing class assignments.

One was of George Washington crossing the Potomac, saying silly things shown in balloon captions over his head.

Sandy did all of these things in spite of a handicap. When she was three, she became ill with polio, a virus that destroys nerve passages between the brain and muscles of the body. The disease paralyzed Sandy's left shoulder and weakened her left arm so much that she had to adapt from being left-handed to using her right hand.

Because of her injury, Sandy felt different from other children. The injury was not obvious, thanks to physical therapy, but Sandy knew it was there. From this experience she became aware of the difference between appearances and reality—between how things look and how they really are. Sandy did not look handicapped, but she was. Even today, she cannot use her left arm to lift heavy things above her head.

Sandy was born in Quincy, Massachusetts, on September 11, 1946. Her father, Walter, ran the family gas station and garage. Her mother, Dorothy, was a nurse. Sandy is the oldest of four children. When she was eight, her father began working as an executive for the Shell Oil Company. Each time he was promoted, the family moved—from Massachusetts to Maine to Connecticut. When Sandy was a teenager, his work took the family to southern California.

Sandy remembers how different southern California was from anywhere she had ever been. The sun shone almost every day, and the bright colors of flowers and of red-roofed adobe houses made an impression on her. Some of those vivid colors are in the photographs Sandy makes today.

One summer, Sandy got a job as a waitress at Disneyland. As a child, she had enjoyed comic books, cartoons, and Disney movies. As a teenager working at Walt Disney's amusement park, Sandy saw how convincing fantasy could be to people of all ages. Anything was possible in the make-believe world of Walt Disney.

Looking back, Sandy sees that many experiences she had when she was growing up contributed to the artwork she now makes. But when she was young, she never imagined she would become an artist. It was not until she attended Smith College, a school for women in Massachusetts, that she discovered how much she liked learning about art and art history. For her junior year, Sandy studied art history in Paris at famous places like the Louvre museum and the Sorbonne, part of the University of Paris.

A year after she graduated from Smith College, Sandy enrolled in graduate school at the University of Iowa. There, she studied painting and sculpture and became interested in filmmaking. Once, Sandy shot a horror movie starring her brother as a dead man who rises from the grave. Sandy made him appear so ghostly that when police drove by and saw him dozing in a car during a break in the filming, they stopped to investigate. They thought he was dead! Sandy had already learned how to make staged scenes look convincingly real.

Sandy finished graduate school with a Master

of Fine Arts degree in painting. (However, most of her work combined different media, such as sculpture, sewing, and spray paint.) She then taught art at the University of Hartford in Connecticut for many years. That is where she met her husband, Al Baccili, a martial arts expert and maker of musical instruments. When Sandy was not teaching, she painted and drew.

During the summer of 1978, Sandy tried an experiment. Using Al's camera, she photographed still lifes she had arranged from objects in the house trailer where she and Al lived. One set-up was of peaches reflected in the shiny side of an aluminum toaster. Sandy liked how the camera made the peaches appear real in a way a painting or drawing never could. She wanted to see how other everyday things would look in pictures. That year, Sandy began photographing in earnest.

Throughout her training in art and art history, Sandy had never taken a class in photography. From her experience with making films, she understood the workings of the camera, but she had to teach herself how to make prints in the darkroom. She asked photographer friends for advice and got tips from the local camera store. Sandy picked up the rest of the technical information she needed as she went along.

Among her early images are color photographs of frozen food. In *Peas on a Plate* (1979), she carefully lined up frozen peas to form a diamond on a brightly colored party plate. The plate sits on decorative paper used to cover the inside of kitchen cabinets. The peas are laid out so perfectly that we see them as elements in a pattern, not as food.

To get inspiration for these pictures, Sandy looked at color photo ads of food in magazines. The artificial and theatrical quality of these images fascinated her. The advertisements showed products carefully set up in a studio to look their best. Sandy knows, however, that appearances are deceiving. A product never looks as good at home as it does in the ad. Just as Sandy spoofed class assignments with cartoons when she was a girl, she now made pictures that poked fun at the exaggerated staging of advertising photographs.

Sandy was one of several American artists working in the 1970s and 1980s who used images from magazines, newspapers, and advertisements as inspiration for their art. Like Sandy, many of these artists were trained in arts other than photography. Painters and sculptors, who created their art from scratch, now applied the same approach to photography. Rather than look at the world around them for something to photograph, they constructed scenes to put in front of the camera. For them, photography was an act of invention. Few people, however, went as far as Sandy did in bringing make-believe to life on film.

For example, starting in 1979, Sandy began

Peas on a Plate, 1979

Hangers, 1979

arranging entire rooms to be photographed. In one picture, titled *Hangers,* she painted a room in her studio bright yellow and pink, then covered it from top to bottom with blue clothes hangers. Everything is set up for the camera's point of view: the hangers are carefully placed to outline the chairs as though the scene is flat and the hangers were drawn in position. The man in pajamas stepping into the room seems unaware of the strangeness of his surroundings. This is true in many of Sandy's pictures. The people in the pictures do not appear to see the same things we, the viewers, do. We get the feeling Sandy is showing us something special, something only the camera can see.

A year later, Sandy made one of her best-known photographs, *Radioactive Cats.* She started by spending hours thinking about how to make a photograph of a room full of cats. How many cats would there be? What would they be doing? What kind of room would they be in? Once Sandy had an idea of how the picture would look, she got to work.

First, she molded twenty-five cats out of chicken wire and plaster and painted them day-glo green. Next, she built a set, like a movie or stage set. She furnished it with a table, two chairs, and a refrigerator she found in a junk shop. Then she painted everything gray, even the radiator, the floor, and the kitchen window. Sandy

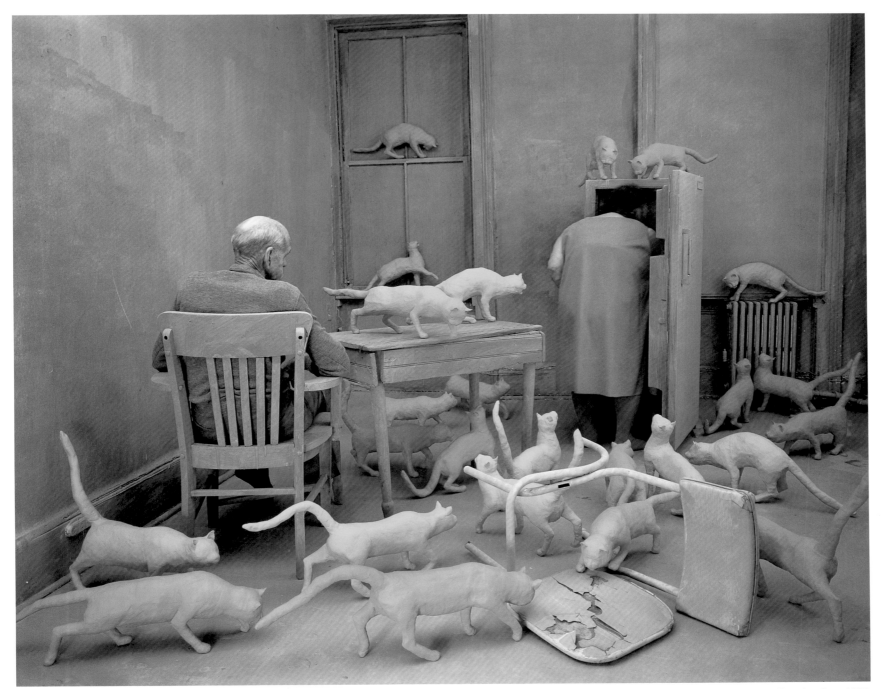

Radioactive Cats, 1980

positioned the cats around the room and brought in two friends to pose for her. She gave them gray clothes to wear and told them where to sit and stand. Sandy loaded the camera with film and, when everything was just right, she took the picture. All of this work, from start to finish, took about six months.

Usually, we think of photographs as showing us something from the world around us. We believe pictures provide proof that a person or place existed or that an event actually happened. Sandy's photograph looks like something from a science fiction movie where cats glow from exposure to radiation. As in Sandy's image of a room covered with blue hangers, her picture of a dingy gray kitchen overrun by neon-green cats is not like any photograph we have seen before.

For a piece Sandy made in 1981, called *Revenge of the Goldfish*, she made one hundred and twenty goldfish out of ceramic clay and painted them deep orange. She hung dozens of them from thin wire in a bright blue bedroom. The hanging fish look as though they are swimming in the air. The others squirm and squiggle on the furniture or on the floor. The title suggests that the goldfish want to get back at someone. But whom? And what for?

In real life, goldfish are pets we keep in glass bowls so we can watch them swim and eat. Sandy's photograph, however, makes us wonder what might happen if goldfish could swim in the air that we breathe. Would they live in our homes, as they do in Sandy's photograph? Would their "revenge" be to watch us, as we now watch them? When Sandy imagines animals as having thoughts and feelings, she wonders what they would think. Through her art, she explores how our world might look through the eyes of the animals she photographs.

To make her pictures, Sandy uses a large camera that produces big negatives. The bigger the negative, the sharper and clearer the image is when the print is made. Sandy produces huge prints—about three feet high by four feet long. The size and descriptive detail of Sandy's photographs add to their power. She also uses a photographic paper that emphasizes the lush, brilliant color of her sets.

In a gallery or museum, Sandy often exhibits a photograph alongside the set she built for it. When the two are next to each other, people see how they are different. The magic of Sandy's art is in the way photography transforms her made-up scenes. The original sets are obviously staged, but the photographs give us a new and delightfully haunting reality.

In 1992, thirteen years after she made *Peas on a Plate*, Sandy went back to photographing food. In an image called *Atomic Love*, she used raisins as atoms, the tiny particles that make up

Revenge of the Goldfish, 1981, and detail

Detail from *Atomic Love*, 1992

the universe. Everything in the yellow room, including a family of mannequins and the clothes of two live models, is densely covered with raisins. But instead of building matter, which is what atoms do, the raisins in this photograph have taken over the room. The live models look surprised and a little concerned at what they see. (This is unlike the reaction of people in Sandy's earlier pictures, where they are unaware of the strange things around them.)

What does the title of this picture mean? Is Sandy saying that love can feel suffocating and take over people's lives, as the raisins have taken over the room? Or does she mean that just as atoms make up our world, love, too, is the basis for everything? Sandy leaves the interpretation up to us.

Also in 1992, Sandy made an image called *Spirituality in the Flesh* (see p. 48). Here, she smeared the wall and floor of her studio with raw hamburger. The entire set, including a mannequin and the stool she sits on, is the pebbled pink of uncooked meat. By using food, which decays and rots, Sandy reminds us of how the camera stops and preserves time. Twenty-four hours after this picture was taken, the meat had turned brown and the set looked completely different, but Sandy's photograph remains unchanged.

Spirituality in the Flesh and *Atomic Love* are dramatic examples of Sandy's persistence and

Atomic Love, 1992

47

Spirituality in the Flesh,
1992

resolve. (Imagine how long it took to press hamburger onto the walls or glue raisins, one by one, onto everything in the set!) Although each of her pieces takes months to make, Sandy enjoys the time and effort that go into them. She views making pictures as part play, part hard work, and she takes both very seriously. One of the great pleasures of her life, Sandy says, is solving problems and meeting challenges.

Over the past ten years, Sandy has become well known for her zany photographs in which animals and foodstuffs reign. Her success is due in part to her resourcefulness. Sandy uses all her skills—as sculptor, painter, cartoonist, and designer—in staging the scenes she photographs. The final image, though, seems to come from the magical world of make-believe. As in a trip to Disneyland, we walk away knowing that we have been somewhere extraordinary. Sandy Skoglund has taken us on a tour of her imagination.

LORNA SIMPSON

Lorna Simpson in 1991

LORNA SIMPSON is an only child, born in Brooklyn, New York, on August 13, 1960. Her father, Elian, is a retired social worker, and her mother, Eleanor, is a medical secretary. When Lorna was a girl, she often went to museums and to the theater with her parents. She loved to look at paintings, and she remembers how exciting it was to see characters brought to life on stage. At an early age, she developed a deep appreciation for art and theater.

Lorna was raised during the civil rights movement, a time in American history when

African-Americans fought for equal rights and for an end to racial segregation. During childhood, she became aware of black America's struggle for equality. An avid reader, Lorna also read books written by African-American authors about the black experience. Respect for all people is the basis of the art she makes today.

Lorna got her first camera when she was nine, from a special offer on a tissue box. She was home in bed with a cold and using lots of tissues when she sent away for the free camera. With it, she photographed family outings and vacations.

Lorna took her first photography class at the High School for Art and Design in New York City. Later, she enrolled in college at New York's School of Visual Arts. Lorna thought she would someday be a painter or a designer for advertisements. But after a year, she realized she was spending more time in the darkroom than in the painting studio. From then on she focused her time and energy on photography.

While in college, Lorna worked as an intern in the education department at the Studio Museum in Harlem. (Harlem is a part of New York City where many African-American and Latino people live.) The museum specializes in promoting work by African-American and Latino artists. As part of its activities, the museum invites artists to work in a studio on its grounds. This program gave Lorna an opportunity to see how professional artists work—an important experience for an art student. Lorna made many friends at the Studio Museum. When she was still in her twenties, she became part of a community of artists that has encouraged her throughout her education and her career.

In college, Lorna made black and white photographs of people on the streets and subways of New York. After a while, though, she felt that something was missing. She wanted her pictures to raise questions about how society functions, not just show the way things look. In 1982, she entered graduate school at the University of California in San Diego, determined to change her style of photographing.

Lorna wanted to make photographs about African-American history and about her experience as an African-American woman. But she was not sure how to do this. For three years, she experimented. Finally, she settled on a method that she has used ever since. To talk about social issues, Lorna combines photographs she sets up in the studio with words or stories she has written. The pieces are dramatic and theatrical. Like Sandy Skoglund, she invents scenes to put before the camera.

A piece Lorna made in 1986 is called *Waterbearer*. In it, a black woman wearing a shapeless white shift stands with her back to the camera. With her left hand, she pours water out

SHE SAW HIM DISAPPEAR BY THE RIVER
THEY ASKED HER TO TELL WHAT HAPPENED
ONLY TO DISCOUNT HER MEMORY.

Waterbearer, 1986

of an old-fashioned metal pitcher. With her right hand, she pours water out of a plastic jug. The water containers from two different generations suggest that the picture is about days past and the present time. Underneath the photograph Lorna added the words:

> She saw him disappear by the river
> They asked her to tell what happened
> Only to discount her memory.

Waterbearer comes from a story Lorna was once told about a man who disappeared by a river under mysterious circumstances. Rather than try to illustrate the story she heard, Lorna gives us a mysterious story of her own. Because the text starts with the word "she" and the photograph is of a woman, we think of the woman in the picture as the one in the text. We imagine she once saw something happen by a river. But when she told what she saw, she was not believed. She alone bears the burden and the truth of what she saw. This piece makes us think about the loneliness and the injustice of not being believed.

The meaning of *Waterbearer*, or any of Lorna's pieces, is not obvious. To encourage different readings, Lorna makes her pieces vague. They tell only part of the message. It is up to us to fill in the rest. That is the fun and the challenge of Lorna's art. She starts the conversation with her staged pictures and her mysterious writing. We

Stereo Styles, 1988

finish it by adding our own interpretations.

Stereo Styles, a piece Lorna made in 1988, talks about how women are classified, or labeled, in fashion magazines by the way they look. *Stereo Styles* contains ten photographs of the back of the same woman's head. The only thing that changes from one image to the next is her hair style. The words that accompany the piece are those used in fashion and advertising—"daring," "sensible," "severe," "long and silky," "boyish," "ageless," "silly," "magnetic," "country fresh," "sweet." As we read, we try to match each one of the phrases to one of the pictures. Which woman is "ageless"?

Which one is "sweet"? Is the woman with daisies in her hair "country fresh"?

The pictures and words in *Stereo Styles* tell us nothing about the woman who posed for the photograph. Instead, the piece reminds us how demeaning it is to reduce an entire personality to one word or phrase. It shows us how such descriptions of people do not tell anything about a person's true character.

In *Stereo Styles*, we do not know who the model is. This is true of all of Lorna's images. Over and over we see the back of the sitter, but we do not see her face. Lorna explains that these

53

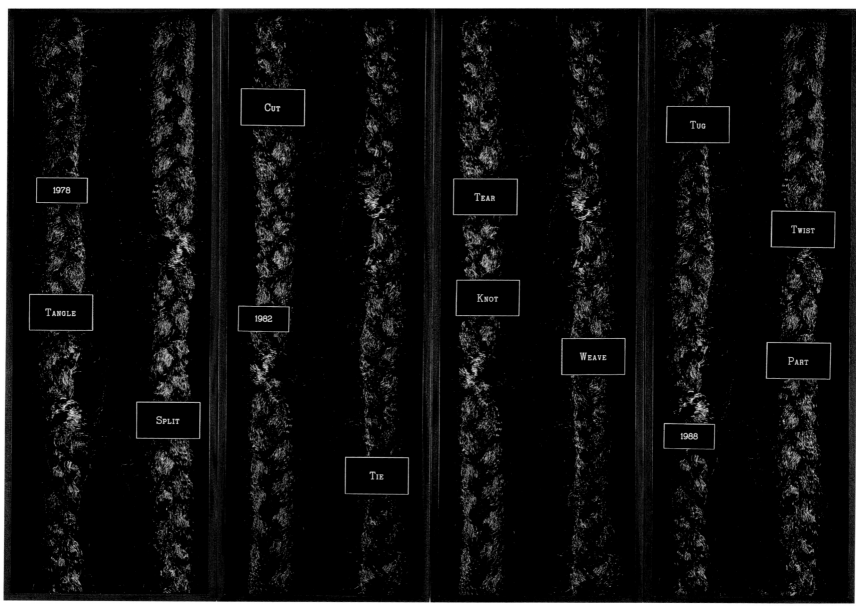

1978–88, 1990

are not the kind of portraits we are used to, where the person in the photograph can be recognized. Since each model is anonymous, we wonder who we might be looking at. It could be someone we know. It could even be you.

There are times that Lorna does not use a model. When she was a girl and she needed a haircut, her mother braided her hair, cut the braid, and then attached a tag marked with the date. The braid of hair marked time and Lorna's growth. In her piece *1978-88*, Lorna lets braids of hair tell a story about a painful relationship. She tied together braid extensions to form a time line. Along it are plaques with words that describe what can be done to hair: "tangle," "split," "cut," "tie," "tear," "knot," "weave," "tug," "twist," "part." Lorna says that the words also describe what can happen between two people over a ten-year period. After a decade of tangling with each other, of being tied to one another, and tugging and tearing at each other, the two people Lorna is thinking of part.

Hair is an important element in many of Lorna's pieces. She knows that people often judge others by their hair styles, by their skin color, or by how they are dressed. She was thinking of this when she made *Flipside* (see p. 56). On the left is a photograph of the back of a black woman's head. She has short, unstraightened hair. On the right is a photograph of the back, or flip side, of an African mask, which is a symbol of African tradition. Lorna chose a mask in the shape of a human head, with hair that flips at the bottom. The flip resembles the style of straightened hair that was popular with African-American women before the civil rights movement of the 1960s. Underneath the two photographs is written "the neighbors were suspicious of her hairstyle."

Flipside comes from an event in Lorna's childhood. When Lorna was about ten years old, her mother began to wear her hair in an Afro (a natural, unstraightened cut that is round in shape). In the 1960s, the Afro became a symbol of the African-American struggle for equal rights and political power. At the time, the Simpsons lived in a working-class black community in Queens, New York. To the neighbors, Lorna's mother's Afro was a political statement. It looked radical. It made them question who she was.

Lorna looks back on this and sees that people were judging her mother by her hair style, not by her character. When we judge others on their appearances or ethnic origins, we do not see who they really are. We lump them into groups and deny them their individuality. Worst of all, we lose the chance to learn from our differences.

In 1991, Lorna was invited to participate in an exhibition in Charleston, South Carolina. For the show, she created *Five Rooms*, an installation about slavery. (An installation is artwork made for

 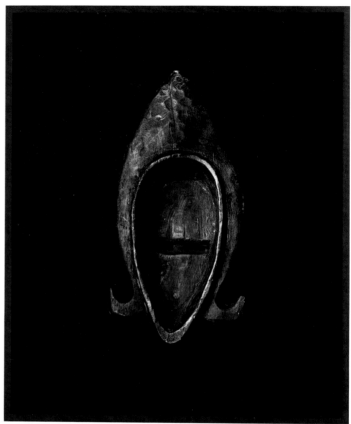

the neighbors were
suspicious of her hairstyle

Flipside, 1991

exhibition in a particular place. It is taken apart once the show is over.) Up until then, Lorna had made all her art on her own. This time, she asked actress, singer, and composer Alva Rogers to collaborate with her. Together, they filled five rooms in a town house in Charleston that was once home to enslaved Africans.

In one room, big bottles of water sat on pedestals. Each was labeled with the name of an actual slave ship. Under the name was the ship's port of origin in Africa and the number of African adults and children on board. In the same room, four photographs hung in a row on the wall. On the far left and far right were pictures of a black woman with her back turned. In one, she wore a white shirt; in the other, her back was bare. Between, two photographs showed a single braid of hair stretching left and right. Through audio speakers, the room was filled with songs sung by Alva and the distant sound of ocean waves.

Lorna once read that during the terrible voyage from Africa, women often braided each other's hair to comfort one another. In Lorna's installation, the two women appeared linked, frame to frame, by the single braided chain of hair. The hair also stands for the connection between all African-Americans and their ancestors.

The other four rooms in *Five Rooms* were arranged according to themes. One theme was

One room from *Five Rooms*, 1991

slave revolts. Another was the growth of the rice industry in the South and how this was used to justify the importation of slaves. A third room was devoted to trees of the area. In that one, visitors heard Alva sing "Strange Fruit," a song that mourns the lynching of blacks in the South. Blues singer Billie Holliday sang this song in the 1930s. The last room told about the high rate of infant deaths among poor African-Americans during slave times and today.

To make this installation, Lorna and Alva decided on everything together, from what music was played to how things would be hung or placed in each room. This was a rewarding experience for Lorna. It took her out of her usual working routine and expanded her thinking. It also encouraged her to use photographs with other arts, like music.

Lorna enjoyed combining media so much that she decided to do it again. In 1993, she asked a glass artist, Kim Petro, to create wishbones for an installation Lorna made about wishing. In this piece, two hundred glass wishbones hung on a gallery wall. Underneath were photographs of broken wishbones. Lorna added the text "Clearly, if you got what you wished you know you'd end up wanting another wish." She repeated the text along the wall to emphasize her message.

Here, Lorna looked at human nature—at the hopes and desires everyone has. We all make wishes—on wishbones, on pennies tossed in fountains, and on stars. But if what Lorna says is true, the cycle of wishing is endless. Even if our wishes come true, we want more. Her two hundred glass wishbones were hung as a reminder that wishing results in more wishing.

Lorna's installation of wishbones is one of many pieces she has exhibited in museums and galleries throughout the United States over the past few years. In that time, two books about her art have been published, she made a billboard in Copenhagen, Denmark, as part of a public art project, and she has received many awards. These are impressive accomplishments for an artist who is only in her mid-thirties. Today, Lorna divides her time between making new work and traveling to foreign countries, where she talks to students and the public about her art.

When Lorna looks back on how she got to where she is, she feels that she was given many opportunities to grow and develop by friends and artists who believed in her. As a child, Lorna learned that each person is an important part of a larger world, and everyone has something valuable to contribute. By making art about prejudice, loneliness, injustice, and hope, Lorna contributes to our awareness of human failings and to our understanding of ourselves.

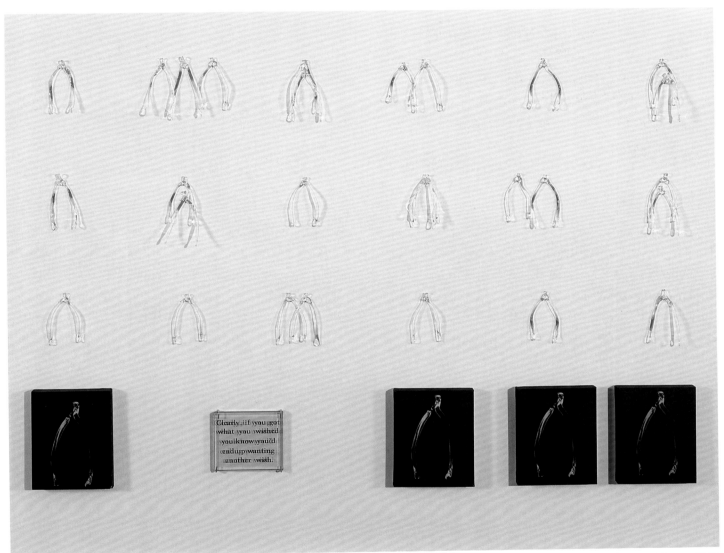

Within the image: "Clearly, if you got what you wished you know you'd end up wanting another wish."

Detail from *Wishbones*, 1993

59

PHOTO CREDITS

Julia Margaret Cameron

6   *Julia Margaret Cameron and Her Children Charles and Henry, c.* 1860. Attributed to the circle of Charles Dodgson. Michael and Jane Wilson Collection. Photo credit: Miki Slingsby.

9   *Annie, My First Success,* 1864. Albumen print from wet collodion negative, 7 1/2 x 5 1/2 in. Gernsheim Collection, Harry Ransom Humanities Research Center, University of Texas at Austin, 964:037:102.

10   *Sir John Herschel,* 1867. Carbon print, 14 x 10 3/4 in. The Art Institute of Chicago, Alfred Stieglitz Collection, 1949.883. Photograph © 1994, The Art Institute of Chicago. All rights reserved.

11   *Alfred Tennyson,* 1865. Albumen print from wet collodion negative, 19 1/4 x 14 1/2 in. Gernsheim Collection, Harry Ransom Humanities Research Center, University of Texas at Austin, 964:037:055.

13   *Pomona,* 1872. Albumen print from wet collodion negative, 13 1/2 x 10 1/2 in. The Royal Photographic Society, Bath.

14   *Call, I follow, I follow, let me die! c.* 1867. Albumen print from wet collodion negative, 13 7/8 x 10 3/8 in. Gift of Mrs. J. D. Cameron Bradley. Courtesy, Museum of Fine Arts, Boston.

15   *Ceylon, c.* 1875. Albumen print from wet collodion negative, 10 3/4 x 9 in. The Art Institute of Chicago, Harriott A. Fox Fund, 1970.843. Photograph © 1994, The Art Institute of Chicago. All rights reserved.

Margaret Bourke-White

16   *Margaret Bourke-White in High-Altitude Flying Suit,* 1943. *Life* Magazine © Time Warner.

18   *Blast Furnace Operator with "Mud Gun," Otis Steel Company, c.* 1927-28. Gelatin silver print, 13 x 10 in. Courtesy of the Margaret Bourke-White Estate. Photo courtesy Syracuse University Library.

20   *Dam at Fort Peck, Montana,* 1936. (First cover of *Life.*) Margaret Bourke-White, *Life* Magazine © Time Warner.

21   *Boy in Chair, Belmont, Florida,* 1936-37. Gelatin silver print, 13 7/8 x 11 in. Margaret Bourke-White, *Life* Magazine © Time Warner. Photo courtesy Syracuse University Library.

23   *Buchenwald, Germany, the Day after Liberation, April, 1945.* Gelatin silver print, 16 x 20 7/8 in. Margaret Bourke-White, *Life* Magazine © Time Warner.

24   *Gandhi, India,* 1946. Gelatin silver print, 11 x 14 in. Margaret Bourke-White, *Life* Magazine © Time Warner.

27   *Gold Miners, Johannesburg, South Africa,* 1950. Gelatin silver print, 32 x 22 in. Margaret Bourke-White, *Life* Magazine © Time Warner.

Flor Garduño

28   Flor Garduño in 1986. © Adriano Heitmann.

30   *Kings of Canes, Tulancingo, Mexico,* 1981. Gelatin silver print, 16 x 20 in. © 1981 Flor Garduño.

31 *Cloud, Jocotitlán, Mexico*, 1982. Gelatin silver print, 16 x 20 in. © 1982 Flor Garduño.

33 *The Woman, Juchitán, Mexico*, 1987. Gelatin silver print, 16 x 20 in. © 1987 Flor Garduño.

34 *Eagle Knight, Jalpán, Mexico*, 1986. Gelatin silver print, 20 x 16 in. © 1986 Flor Garduño.

35 *Sixto, Altos de la Paz, Bolivia*, 1990. Gelatin silver print, 20 x 16 in. © 1990 Flor Garduño.

36 *Basket of Light, Sumpango, Guatemala*, 1989. Gelatin silver print, 20 x 16 in. © 1989 Flor Garduño. (Also frontispiece.)

Sandy Skoglund

38 Sandy Skoglund at work in 1991. © Andrew Eccles/Outline.

41 *Peas on a Plate*, 1979. Cibachrome print, 22 x 28 in. © 1979 Sandy Skoglund, courtesy Janet Borden Inc., New York.

42 *Hangers*, 1979. Cibachrome print, 30 x 40 in. © 1979 Sandy Skoglund, courtesy Janet Borden Inc., New York.

43 *Radioactive Cats*, 1980. Cibachrome print, 30 x 40 in. © 1980 Sandy Skoglund, courtesy Janet Borden Inc., New York.

45 *Revenge of the Goldfish*, 1981, and detail. Cibachrome print, 30 x 40 in. © 1981 Sandy Skoglund, courtesy Janet Borden Inc., New York.

47 *Atomic Love*, 1992. Cibachrome print, 40 x 60 in. © 1992 Sandy Skoglund, courtesy Janet Borden Inc., New York. (Detail, p. 46.)

48 *Spirituality in the Flesh*, 1992. Cibachrome print, 35 3/4 x 28 in. © 1992 Sandy Skoglund, courtesy Janet Borden Inc., New York.

Lorna Simpson

50 Lorna Simpson in 1991. Photo © Timothy Greenfield-Sanders.

52 *Waterbearer*, 1986. Gelatin silver print, one engraved plastic plaque, 41 3/4 x 79 1/4 x 2 1/4 in. © 1986 Lorna Simpson.

53 *Stereo Styles*, 1988. Ten Polaroid prints, ten engraved plastic plaques, 66 x 116 in. © 1988 Lorna Simpson. Photo credit: Ellen Page Wilson.

54 *1978-88*, 1990. Four gelatin silver prints, thirteen engraved plastic plaques, 49 x 70 in. © 1990 Lorna Simpson. Photo credit: Ellen Page Wilson.

56 *Flipside*, 1991. Two gelatin silver prints, one engraved plastic plaque, 51 1/2 x 70 in. © 1991 Lorna Simpson. Photo credit: Ellen Page Wilson.

57 One room from *Five Rooms*, 1991. Room installation created for "Places with a Past," the Spoleto Festival, U.S.A., Charleston, South Carolina. Glass water bottles, wooden stools, four Polaroid prints, engraved plastic plaques. Dimensions variable. © 1991 Lorna Simpson.

59 Detail from *Wishbones*, 1993. Glass wishbones, engraved plastic plaques, gelatin silver prints on linen, 80 1/2 in. x 19 ft. © 1993 Lorna Simpson.

SELECTED BIBLIOGRAPHY

Julia Margaret Cameron

Ford, Colin. *The Cameron Collection.* London: Van Nostrand Reinhold, 1975.

Gernsheim, Helmut. *Julia Margaret Cameron: Her Life and Photographic Work.* New York: Aperture, 1975.

Hill, Brian. *Julia Margaret Cameron: A Victorian Family Portrait.* New York: St. Martin's Press, 1973.

Hopkinson, Amanda. *Julia Margaret Cameron.* London: Virago Press, 1986.

Ovenden, Graham, ed. *A Victorian Album: Julia Margaret Cameron and Her Circle.* New York: Da Capo Press, 1975.

Powell, Tristram, ed. *Victorian Photographs of Famous Men and Fair Women by Julia Margaret Cameron.* Boston: David R. Godine, 1973.

Weaver, Mike. *Julia Margaret Cameron, 1815-1879.* Boston: Little, Brown, 1984.

_____. *Whisper of the Muse: The Overstone Album and Other Photographs by Julia Margaret Cameron.* Malibu, Calif.: The J. Paul Getty Museum, 1986.

Margaret Bourke-White

Bourke-White, Margaret. *Portrait of Myself.* New York: Simon and Schuster, 1963.

_____. *Shooting the Russian War.* New York: Simon and Schuster, 1943.

_____, and Erskine Caldwell. *You Have Seen Their Faces: American Farmers and the Rise of Agribusiness.* New York: Modern Age Books, 1937.

Callahan, Sean, ed. *The Photographs of Margaret Bourke-White.* New York: Bonanza Books, 1972.

Goldberg, Vicki. *Bourke-White,* exhibition catalogue. New York: International Center for Photography, 1988.

_____. *Margaret Bourke-White: A Biography.* New York: Harper & Row, 1986.

Silverman, Jonathan. *For the World to See: The Life of Margaret Bourke-White.* New York: Viking Press, 1983.

Flor Garduño

Galeano, Eduardo. "Flor Garduño: Fotoessay." *Du 1* (January 1992), pp. 10-76. (Zurich.)

Garduño, Flor. *Flor Garduño Bestiarium.* Zurich: Argentum, 1987.

_____. *Magia del juego eterno: Fotografias de Flor Garduño [Magic of the Eternal Game: Photographs of Flor Garduño].* Oaxaca, Mexico: Guchachi' Reza A. C. Juchitán, 1985.

_____. *Witnesses of Time: Flor Garduño.* New York: Thames and Hudson, 1992.

Other Images: Other Realities: Mexican Photography Since 1930, exhibition catalogue. Houston, Texas: Rice University, 1990.

Velarde, Ramon Lopez. *La suave patria [My Sweet Homeland].* Mexico: Teléfonos de Mexico S.A., 1983.

Sandy Skoglund

Eauclaire, Sally. *The New Color Photography*. New York: Abbeville Press, 1981.

Grundberg, Andy, and Marvin Heiferman. *The Indomitable Spirit: Photographers and Friends United against AIDS*. New York: Harry N. Abrams, 1990.

Grundberg, Andy, and Kathleen McCarthy Gauss. *Photography and Art*. New York: Abbeville Press, 1987.

Hoy, Anne. *Fabrications: Staged, Altered, and Appropriated Photographs*. New York: Abbeville Press, 1987.

Indiana, Gary. "Home." *Aperture* 127 (Spring 1992), pp. 56-63.

Raven, Arlene. *In the Last Hour: Sandy Skoglund Photographs and Sculpture 1979-1992*, exhibition catalogue. Norman, Okla: Fred Jones, Jr. Museum of Art, 1992.

Richardson, Nan. "Sandy Skoglund: Wild at Heart." *Art News* 90 (April 1991), pp. 115-19.

Skoglund, Sandy. "Spirituality in the Flesh, A Project for *Art Forum* by Sandy Skoglund." *Art Forum* 30 (February 1992), pp. 72-73.

Smith, Joshua P. *The Photography of Invention: American Pictures of the 1980's*. Cambridge, Mass.: The MIT Press, 1989.

Lorna Simpson

Berger, Maurice, Simon Watson, and John S. Weber. *Dissent, Difference and the Body Politic*. Portland, Oreg.: Portland Art Museum, 1993.

Gelover, Cheryl. *Lorna Simpson*. Elkins Park, Pa.: Tyler School of Art, Temple University, 1993.

Hillings, Valerie, and Lisa Constantino. *In Search of Self*. Durham, N.C.: Duke University Museum of Art, 1993.

Larson, Kay. *American Art Today: Clothing as Metaphor*. Miami, Fla:. The Art Museum, Florida International University, 1993.

Soloman-Godeau, Abigail. *Mistaken Identities*. Santa Barbara, Calif.: The Regents of the University of California, 1993.

Willis, Deborah. *Lorna Simpson: Untitled 54*. San Francisco: The Friends of Photography, 1992.

Willis-Thomas, Deborah. *Black Photographers, 1840-1940*. New York: Garland Publishing, 1985.

Wright, Beryl J., and Saidiya V. Hartman. *Lorna Simpson: For the Sake of the Viewer*. New York: Universe Publishing; Chicago: Museum of Contemporary Art, 1992.

I would like to thank all of the people at Albert Whitman who contributed to the production of this book: Kathy Tucker, for inviting me to write it; Karen Campbell, for its elegant design; Christy Grant, for her research assistance; and most of all, Abby Levine, for her insightful reading of the text and for her extraordinary editorial gifts.

In my research for this book, I turned to many books and articles (some are listed in the bibliography). In addition, I interviewed the three living photographers, Flor, Sandy, and Lorna. I would like to express my special thanks to them for the time and energy they put into this project, and above all, for doing the work that gave me so much to write about. S.W.

Library of Congress Cataloging in Publication Data

Wolf, Sylvia.
Focus: five women photographers / by Sylvia Wolf.
p. cm.
Includes bibliographical references (pp. 62-63).
ISBN 0-8075-2531-6
1. Cameron, Julia Margaret Pattle, 1815-1879—Juvenile literature.
2. Bourke-White, Margaret, 1904-1971—Juvenile literature.
3. Garduño, Flor—Juvenile literature. 4. Skoglund, Sandy, 1946-
—Juvenile literature. 5. Simpson, Lorna—Juvenile literature.
6. Women photographers—Biography—Juvenile literature.
[1. Photographers. 2. Women—Biography.] I. Title.
TR139.W65 1994   94-1416
770'.92'2—dc20   CIP
[B]   AC